High Shelf

High Shelf XXXIII. August 2021.
Portland, Oregon.
Copyright 2021, High Shelf Press

ISBN: 978-1-952869-38-9

Cover Image by Alexx Mayes
Design and Layout by C. M. Tollefson
Editing by David Seung & C. M. Tollefson

With special thanks to:
Eric Hoskins, Megan Kim, & River Elizabeth Hall.

High Shelf Press reserves all rights to the material contained herein for the contributors protection; upon publication, all rights revert to the artists.

High Shelf XXXIII
August 2021

"...a shuddering phone line
wrapped in a hurricane
holding between two poles across a cornfield the length of the sunset.

Delicate... "

Grayson Thompson

"... And now, of course,
we're all too poor
for painters..."

Julia Gibson

Table Of Contents

Vague Body, Name Your Weapon — 9
Becca Carson

Cardinal — 10
Corie Rosen

we were too poor for a real heirloom — 11
Quinton Jordebrek

Welcome to the Future — 12
Alexx Mayes

Down by the River — 18
Stella Robertson

Poem set to one hundred metronomes — 19
Laura Kenney

When you used to say my name like that — 21
Grayson Thompson

Behind Glass — 22
Gabriela De Paz

What If — 34
Shantha J. Bunyan

You Will Need Food for the Journey — 35
Trapper Markelz

Urbex Stained Glass — 36
Danny Rebb

ANATOMY OF HOOKAH — 51
Bingh

Nomad Stills — 52
Christopher Ghattas

Last Chance for Sandwich Bread — 68
Julia Gibson

Clock Struck 13 — 70
Cheng Tim Tim

A Confusing Path — 72
Nichole Spates

Mild Symptoms — 77
Andrew Tye

For The Birds	78
JoeAnn Hart	
Fear of Flight	80
Hannah Maureen Holden	
Ekphrastic Challenge	86
Greg Turlock & Josephine Pino	

Vague Body, Name Your Weapon

Becca Carson

Vague body, name your weapon
and I will meet you in the cerebellar morning
tundra fresh or hypothermic
to finally settle this: with permanence
out of the question, I'm hoping to avoid heaven
and request instead anything not labeled FOREVER—
because nothing lasts *always* not even oceans or
glaciers or lunar particles blasted into galactic
shrapnel or any of those other things
you can't see but know could be
pulled straight through you in the MRI machine.

Like God, maybe. The God you learned about
at summer camp: all knowing, score keeping bastard
watching you always. *Let his love fill you
and wash away your sins* I think the song went
but no holy light reached you right
and in the grainy camp showers—
your awkward body corralled by slimy plastic curtains
under the stream of fish-smelling water—

you imagined
him watching.

God, you know, a very old man, and
You couldn't cover yourself fast enough
so you slipped, crumpled into bad angles
over the sucking mouth of a gritty drain,
fingers sinking into a large wet knot of dark hair.
You imagined it as sin— loose, unraveling, filling
your entire unspent body until you choked
and threw up
with God and all the good church girls
watching
through the film of
the furred plastic curtain.

Cardinal

Corie Rosen

You must get busy being born
or you must get busy dying
that's what the songs tell us
and the songs are never wrong

I want to busy myself with birth, with all that newness
to open my mouth and swallow back the rain
to notice the way it falls
cold and merciful against my heart.

To feel the rain on your face is
to live and not be thankless.
Emotion embarrasses us but emotion,
like the rain
is, finally, all there is.

How can I get busy being born when
so much of this life stands behind me?

Already I feel the pull of the day
when I look back and not forward
a day that wants reflection, stillness
a day that wants taking stock.

That day is hemmed by cardinal seams
by fissures where, had I turned this way or that way
I wouldn't be quite here
wouldn't be stepping in from the rain, when I
feel my skin and hair dry again
wouldn't be imagining the pressure of your hand
something I used to know.

If I could begin all over again, even if
I had to once again walk through this rainstorm
maybe I could locate a way of knowing when
a good thing arrives before me
maybe I would find a way to
speak its language
to understand when it says
come in, get dry, get warm.

we were too poor for a real heirloom

Quinton Jordebrek

glass bottles clink against one another filling a black plastic bag
after the sun has pulled the bed sheets to its chest
my eight year old mother wanders their living room making sure each bottle is collected
her mother turns eyes towards the sky
hands her daughter my mother silence and pursed lips
hands her never say no's and what happens here stays here
my mother hands me these same things
with her bruised arms and barely open eyes
tells me not to say anything
my mother speaks quiet speaks slow slurred speech
i babysit the secret in the corner with my one year old sister on my five year old hip
my mother sleeps between my baby sister's screams
i tell her she has to remain quiet

Welcome to the Future

Alexx Mayes

Down by the River

Stella Robertson

The water displays the overcast,
and the deadpan expression of late April,
I sip lukewarm lemonade

as a dog wallows, stomach towards the sky,
city water matting his golden fur

into peaks, which dip into the loose sand
and come out encased.

His legs convulse forward in a transition
that is so seamless I can't know,

until his head is thrown back
and staring me down; unblinking.

I can't remember now if he made a sound,
muted maybe,

by the tennis ball between his teeth, trapped,
even when the man scoops him up by all fours

and says only, don't let the kids see.
I search for the fairness in this

but all I find
is my sweet sixteen, when mom and dad
broke the news, and replaced our dog
with a purple betta fish.

Poem set to one hundred metronomes

Laura Kenney

after Ligeti's Poème Symphonique

To the sound of *Moe Serdtse*
Ruth and I watch wax recede
Into pools   of honey
Upon the windowsill. Nine hollows
Flicker silver as   adagio

Shadows suck vinegar from lips,
As Ruth describes the sound:
One-hundred arms   fall silent
Only in the silence, we know,
We are newly afraid   of dying

Like when Dara stays inside
Amid the cigarette exodus
Like when Ruth's   hexagon
Aligns with the flames
An indelible and   soft shape

The way melting is in these small shapes:
How the rod prays toward entropy
In Dara and Ruth's   fingertips
How Ruth places the rod on their
Open hand and   promises

Entirety, a column collapsing into
Its own dew. Listen: the melody
Of intermittent   agony
Of solids slipping toward liquid
Sublime and prostrated.   Opacity

A suggestion: that the hint
Of time's creep grows softer
That parallel strikes   on skin
Grow lighter, and do so with gradual
And mathematical   certainty

That survival is a making a candle
Of one's palm and enduring it.
The eventual   green blister

Of skin above Ruth's skin after
That night   a lantern,
                          a talisman.

When you used to say my name like that

Grayson Thompson

Building a relationship with someone is

a shuddering phone line
wrapped in a hurricane
holding between two poles across a cornfield the length of the sunset.

Delicate.

As it swings over,
the riptide of stalks reach up
like Christmas trees trying to touch God.

The line snaps like a hallelujah.

The words left unsaid fall hard into the roots of the ocean of golden green.

I swear

everytime a husk breaks I can still hear you say
you love me.

Behind Glass
Gabriela De Paz

What If

Shantha J. Bunyan

You Will Need Food for the Journey

Trapper Markelz

When someone dies, we bring the family food,
a sign of some continued living.
A few days later, my neighbor showed up
on the steps, his eyes wider than I'd seen

holding a plate of manicured chicken wings.
They held in their position, the deft perfection
of a breaded henge that shined,
even on a cloudy afternoon.

His eyes flicked nervous, back and forth
from plate to pupils, and back down the street
to the safety of his pale door where no one passed.
It was Sunday and our teams were playing.

Here, he said, *for the game*. Take this food
for you have my heart, is what I think he meant.
Steel yourself for the battle ahead,
not just this business of downs and messy yards.

This isn't your last supper. *You didn't have to*,
I told him. With a nod, he slowly walked
from the porch and retreated to his house.
I watched him from the sidelight and wondered
if that nod meant he did or didn't have to do it.

Urbex Stained Glass
Danny Rebb

ANATOMY OF HOOKAH
Bingh

In
between
puffs, I'd
place the hose

on the table & jot
down on a
napkin
how I think Walt Whitman would totally go w/ me to one of these joints to
lean & loaf at our ease. When I get home I can put these blades of
shisha
into
the best
possible
order
long
after
the haze
has
cleared,
the
same
way the
drunken
-ness
from
a TJ
bar has
passed
as I
make
my way
back to
the border
in order to have this
shapely thing on the page.
It's curious that the nearly 1,000-pg
Poems for the Millennium, volume 2,
ends w/ the prolegomena. "Tenderly—be not
impatient," whistles old Walt. We are "breathing

freely

thru a soft tube," letting ourselves be wafted before
coming back down to resume wading thru the tome.
"You'll get used to it in time," advises the Caterpillar,
in between puffs, in *Alice's Adventures*.

Nomad Stills

Christopher Ghattas

Last Chance for Sandwich Bread

Julia Gibson

It was too hard, or too boring to paint
the peasants whilst they moved
from shack to shack.
And of course, the royals used
peasants to move for them.
So to capture their philosophical natures,
the Haves paid the painters
to dig up a skull and
do a portrait of them doing
the death dance, which is to say
the dance that has no movement
with the skull the artful partner
or onlooker knowing its power
to get written on the dance card.

And now, of course,
we're all too poor
for painters.
Some of us too poor
or too proud to pay
strangers to witness our piles
of shit into boxes.

We didn't make sandwich bread
as often as we thought we would.
Just one slice we didn't taste
as we could have at the time.
The loaves remind us of
the losses already suffered
because of who we are.
No one can blame us for being human.
I can blame myself though if I lapse
out of touch.

The inhuman whine of the boiler room
drills us awake the last night
before we pay plebeians to toast
our shit-sandwich boxes
and our shit toaster oven box
whose wires we've stoked
with every use for the past year.

I let my partner risk electrical fire
because he didn't want to let go
of even a shitty box
and I didn't have the mercy
to make him.
Now he's sad from looking both
at the flatlining box
and the sandwich bread
it doesn't toast.
So he doesn't look at it. Instead,
moves to move
from one side of the one-room
grave box we've lived in
four years to the other side
the sandwich bread maker.
But at first
he doesn't move.
He is doing the death dance
holding the hulking robot skull
in his hands outstretched.

Clock Struck 13

Cheng Tim Tim

November 2019-2020, Hong Kong

i.
A leather sofa sat at a crossroad, looking inwards at thick crowds.
Their dusty, scraped fingers drew tears from a blasphemous worker

who didn't understand their seething grief, a black creature
charging to tear off the billowing white cloth over where he fell,

that carpark building where no one saw in, and no one saw out.
Stop the world. Tsz-Lok is dead. The street is never the same again.

Come closer: the ticking isn't from anywhere but blunt tools birthing
brick-henges, the architecture of deferral first thing in the morning.

ii.
The few days traffic ground to a halt, a twenty-minute ride
or a three-hour hike away, computer chairs stationed

on the arc of a university footbridge where umbrellas crowned,
overlooking the conglomerate on highway: One placed

a brick. Another followed. Bricks upon bricks were to collapse
under cannon wheels. Would they have pressed onto the ground

the worship, wishes and worries not unlike pebble stacking?
I don't know. I don't think that's the right question to ask.

iii.
She gave me a bag of paper cranes she folded in disquiet.
They sat next to a white helmet under my desk every day,

I lived sandwiched between Tsz Lok's, Yin Lam's death scene.
There's a time when strolling made me feel like a teardrop

hovering in a giant's eye, the way I carry on working, living,
sometimes forgetting until I see messages or ceremonies

in the street. Of course, after a while, there were more police
than mourners and reporters. Intricate, bright altars gave way

to a lone person kneeling down before a few candles, to a
single chrysanthemum taped to the covering structures.

One night, it looked almost like Christmas with sirens' blue,
orange lights on police's backs and photos on a lit cross.

A scattered gathering popped up for a shocking, big thing
that I can't quite name now without research. I was told

that by energy conservation, not a bit of them is gone.
They have just become less orderly. So tell me: What now?

A Confusing Path

Nichole Spates

Mild Symptoms

Andrew Tye

How democracy became the engine of empire is the big-ticket question on everybody's lips: the brutal histories: the bleaching of fact into fiction: white-haired men yammering talking heads to death has been our daily direction but never before like this: there is everything going on right now: my friends and I argue by phone whether the night of the harvest moon was a defining development or another thin thread in the national tapestry of mendacious reality woven for our entertainment: underneath the white-haired moon: I heard a violin stream across time and space: Rome burned: its rolling energy too swiftly careening in earnest search for the space of eternity: anxiety of the modern era: votes cast virtually: gases and plastics and landfills: fact erosion: globalism: terrorism: populism: fascism: capitalism: unequal deaths for unequal peoples in unequal streets: the absolute nonshockorscandal of the FinCEN Files: the absolute terror of being able to do nothing while democracy becomes the ending of empire: the white-haired moon plays its fiddle over fire:

For The Birds

JoeAnn Hart

Payson and Valerie Beckworth collapsed on the cobbled veranda with their gin and tonics. It had been a trying day, what with getting the new bird feeder positioned just so in the rose garden. Valerie's face hurt from having to smile through the ordeal of explaining to Lenny Akers from the service, not once, but twice (as if anyone had to be told at all!) about the gabled end of the feeder lining up visually with the gable of the house. Payson had to practically set the post himself—but that was all behind them now. The two Beckworths were thinking that it really had been worth all the bother.

"Isn't it just smashing?" asked Valerie.

Payson nodded and clinked his ice. "What about bird food?"

"Yes, yes," she said, batting at the air with her open hand, as if his question was something physical that could be pushed away. "It's coming. I sent away for a mix that attracts *just* the sort of birds we want."

Valerie leaned back in her cushioned chaise and pictured the garden maturing that year, exactly as that fey young man from the Landscape Studio had predicted. Right then and there she decided to let Suzanne Hollings know that, if asked, Valerie would not object to having the Shore Garden Club meet at her house in July.

The "Deluxe Songbird Mix" arrived late in June, and Valerie ratcheted the feeder down the pole herself, not trusting the job to Lenny. Soon enough, small, bright birds began to arrive, swooping and chirping, and being perfectly charming. At first, Valerie didn't even mind the mess of hulls under the feeder, but by the end of the week it was with genuine disgust that she discovered white splats on the shiny leaves of her heirloom roses.

Valerie had Lenny hand-wipe each soiled leaf with a damp cloth, but that was not nearly enough. She panicked as more birds arrived everyday, and not the ones she had expected either, but hideous grackles and loud, piercing cowbirds.

"The little beggars will simply have to go elsewhere for a couple of weeks for their handouts," Valerie said to Payson at the end of a very long, very hot day. "We have to give the garden, and my nerves, time to recuperate before the Club date."

The bird seed was swiftly packed away, but the birds gave up hope reluctantly. Because of this, there were some *Rosa* 'Pompon Blanc Parfait' blooms that could not be saved from the digestive ends of the last of the feathered visitors, but Valerie bore it well and wrote it off to the caprice of Mother Nature.

When the thirty members of the Shore Garden Club arrived all went according to plan; Valerie could not have asked for more. The members lavished praise on the grounds and gardens, and especially the feeder. Everyone agreed that the *faux* sapling post really did seem to grow right up out of the dirt. They loved how the feeder's arches echoed the lines of house. It looked as if it had always been there. The club members said a great many things about it, but they were all too polite to mention -- indeed, they were too polite to even notice—that the bird feeder had neither bird nor feed.

Valerie decided she would have these lovely women over again, soon.

Days after the last shrimp salad sandwich was thrown in the trash, and the punch bowl rinsed and put away, Valerie and Payson reminded each other that it was safe to put out the bird food again. Unfortunately, the bag of seed seemed to have been misplaced during the clean-up. The Beckworths both agreed that a new bag was needed, but soon it was one thing after another, and summers were short enough as they were.

Fear of Flight

Hannah Maureen Holden

In times of unease I imagine that I am receiving ministry from Victoria. Victoria is a 71-year-old widow who lives in a large, impeccable house in Katonah, New York. Victoria eats a macrobiotic diet, practices yoga five times a week, and abides by the dictum "less, but better." She wears cashmere turtlenecks and drapey trousers and keeps her hair in an elegant bob. She is the respected and admired matriarch of a clan that consists of several generations of attractive, prosperous, gracious, healthy, and emotionally stable individuals. But at the moment I needed her most, Victoria did not feel near. In fact, I never felt further from Victoria than as I sat in seat D18 on Aerial Airlines flight 2447 with direct service to Dallas.

Before takeoff, my neighbor removed from her purse a plastic envelope of disinfectant wipes. She unlatched her dining tray so that it swung flat and scoured its surface and edges. She pointed to my right arm, which lay on our shared armrest. Her eyebrows arched with expectation. Only after several beats did I realize what her gesture indicated. I folded my arm into my torso like a bird's wing. She wiped the armrest. I felt that to return my arm to the rest would be to dirty it again, so I crossed my arms. My neighbor sanitized her seatbelt buckle.

The mid-winter sun streaming through the window was vivid and bright. I could see that there were two small stains on the hem of my sweater that I had not noticed before I left my apartment. My nails were jagged and at all different lengths. I felt that in these small physical imperfections my derangement had crossed the threshold of my mind and manifested in the world. I then wished I had not thought of boundaries, or the permeability of the internal and the external, because I was reminded of the thinness of the plane's acrylic windows and the metal in which I was immured.

On my tray table was a tomato and mozzarella panini in a brown paper bag marked with the green Starbucks insignia. I looked at the siren's blank eyes and her upturned lips. Was she not a goddess of destruction, a portent of doom that emblazoned tens of thousands of coffeehouses and was reproduced ad infinitum on packaging and merchandise?

The panini, shaped like a brick, was an artifact of a more naive time. In the airport terminal, I had dreamed that on the flight I would not be so gripped by terror that my stomach would knot as if in a violent act of self-digestion. As with all dreams, the clarity of light dispelled it. The panini cooled, and the scent of commercially manufactured lightly toasted Italian bread diffused throughout the cabin. I wondered whether it had not been a kind of assault to subject my fellow passengers to the fragrance of a convenience food, particularly one that I was unlikely to consume for the flight's duration. Had I thought more of Victoria, I would not have been so careless. Snacks that Victoria would bring onto a plane were discreet and odorless, like raw sprouted pili nuts and brown rice cakes.

The flight attendant approached. Before me, she slammed an overhead compartment with brisk rage, then in an instant became dove-gentle as she bent to pick up from the aisle a small plush rabbit. She returned the toy to a toddler.

The attendant arrived at my row. "Please return your tray table to its upright position for takeoff," she said. Here was a double-faced Janus, presiding over the transition from groundedness to flight, bearing responsibility for motion, changes, and time.

For many years I was frightened by the apparent formlessness of my life. However, in the days before my flight, I felt that I had at last uncovered its central idea. That idea was this: any undertaking that seems, at the outset, to be easy, will prove more difficult than you have imagined. Everything will take more time than you anticipated, and will be rife with obstacles that only reveal themselves in the midst of your undertakings. That which you believe will bring happiness will, at best, bring a kind of satisfaction. But that satisfaction will be so mild, so hard-won, and so transitory as to bring into question the merit of your ordeal.

I could not return my tray table to its upright position.

First, I gathered the panini and placed it in my tote bag. The tote bag was decorated with the name of a famous magazine. I had received the bag as a reward for subscribing to the magazine, which arrived in my mailbox every week. There is a tiresome bit among urban liberals that goes something like, "My famous magazine is stacking up on the kitchen table, accusing me of not reading it. While it is December, I intend to get around to reading the issue from mid-October. I cannot throw it away because trees died for this." And so I will resign myself from further elaborating on the particulars of this experience. Oh, except to say, Victoria does not have this problem. Victoria claims to prefer to read books rather than magazines in which a great number of books are discussed (although once when I was cleaning her study I found hidden in a drawer a stack of large-print editions of *Reader's Digest*).

Shoved under the seat of the person seated in the row ahead of me, the tote bag looked grimy and deflated. I was relieved to no longer have to stare into the face of the malevolent green siren, but now considered whether it had been a dirty choice to place food in a bag that I had previously set on a great number of counters, floors, and other surfaces. The sandwich was so close to my black boots, which were ringed with the white residue of sidewalk salt. Undoubtedly the boots were coated in other kinds of filth invisible to the naked eye. I glanced at my neighbor, the one with the sanitizing wipes. She appeared to be in a shallow vertical slumber. The bright sun fell on her closed eyelids, which were webbed with thin pink blood vessels.

I lifted my tray table and attempted to latch it. The latch would not rotate counter-clockwise into place. I changed the angle of my grip and jiggled again. Still, it was motionless. I looked around helplessly. I lowered the tray to focus my energies wholly on rotating the latch. I pinched it with the thumbs, forefingers, and middle fingers of both hands. My hands slipped from the latch, as though it were greased. I gathered the fabric of my sweater around my hand and used it to gain purchase around the latch. The latch still wouldn't budge.

Janus appeared at my side. "We can't take off until you return your tray table to its upright position," she said.

"But I can't," I said. I showed her how the latch would not rotate.

She wrapped her hands around the latch. The manicured almonds of her fingernails glinted in the sun. She attempted to rotate the latch, but it did not move. She persisted, with no success.

"Just a moment," she said.

Passengers in the seats around me muttered in annoyance. As the plane idled near the terminal, the cabin grew hot. The intermingled fragrance of bread and sanitizing alcohol became more intense in this heat. A few rows ahead, I saw the plush rabbit go flying into the aisle. With no one to retrieve his toy, the toddler howled.

Janus returned. In her hand she held what I at first thought was a pair of pliers, but which I realized was a nutcracker. She gripped the latch with the nutcracker and attempted to rotate it.

"No dice," Janus said. "Give it a shot?"

I accepted the nutcracker and tried to rotate the latch. I thought I felt it begin to twist by a few millimeters when the latch snapped completely from its mechanism. It landed in my lap like a severed finger.

The eyes of Janus grew large. Helplessly, I lifted the tray back to its folded position. Of course, when I released it, it fell back to its perpendicular position.

"This is fine," I said. "Don't worry about me." My neighbor's eyes had opened, and she looked at me with annoyance.

"I'm afraid it's not fine," Janus said. "It's FAA regulation that all tray tables must be in the upright position before we move."

"She's right," my neighbor said. "The bylaw is known as Part 121."

"What if we duct tape it closed?" I said.

Janus shook her head. "That's not secure. If the tray falls open, it might obstruct passengers from evacuating in case of emergency."

"60% of airplane crashes take place during takeoffs and landings," my neighbor said.

"I need to inform the pilot of what you've done," Janus said.

Minutes passed. I realized that I should have brought with me a few back issues of the famous magazine. I was counting on the soporific network sitcoms available on the in-flight entertainment system to occupy myself on the plane. But those would be unavailable until we took flight. In the back pocket of the chair in front of me, below the unfolded tray table, were a combination safety-and-menu card, a mail-order catalog, and a magazine published by the airline that I did not want to read.

Above our heads the in-flight intercom system crackled.

"Attention passengers. Your pilot is speaking. Unfortunately, due to a problem with the plane, we will be unable to take off. Passengers are instructed to deboard the plane and return to the terminal. At the terminal, Aerial

Airlines representatives will be on-hand to assist you in rebooking your flight. We apologize for the inconvenience."

The cabin erupted in a collective groan. I felt as though a balloon were rising in my stomach. This feeling, I realized, was elation. I would refund my ticket. I would return to my apartment. I would not hurtle through the air, risking my one and only precious life for the sake of convenience and speed. I grasped the broken latch, a newfound talisman of providence and good fortune.

Once all the passengers had "deboarded," to borrow a graceless neologism, they queued at a service desk. I walked to the furthest part of the terminal and seated myself in the waiting area. I looked through floor-to-ceiling windows at the proceedings on the tarmac and runway. A yellow cart pulled up to the plane that I had just evacuated. Perhaps it would gather from the plane's belly the checked luggage of the other passengers. I preferred to travel lightly, with only my tote bag, which once again seemed a sharp, charming signifier of my devotion to a certain famous magazine that I sometimes got around to reading, but often did not. In the distance, a small white blur took off from the runway at an improbable angle. It wobbled as it launched itself through a curtain of silver clouds.

My appetite had returned. I removed from my tote bag the paper bag containing the panini. Although it had cooled, it tasted okay. I felt a buzz in the tote bag and reached within to retrieve my phone. The caller ID indicated it was Victoria who was trying to reach me.

I declined the call, and selected from the drop-down menu of automated replies, "Sorry, I can't talk right now." I returned my phone to the tote bag and continued eating my sandwich, grateful that both my feet were heavy on the ground.

Screech Owl

Photography by Greg Turlock
Poetry by Josephine Pino

The siren's wail faded as thunder rumbled
and clouds painted the air black.

Smoke rose above the sizzling mass.
The flames dwindled

but the acrid smell remained for days.
I was there when it happened -

the screech of brakes
the violent shatter of glass once, twice...

and the third
accompanied by a scream.

I went hungry that night.
The sound of human fear

pervaded the swamp and the vehicle
landed where *we*

live and die yet it is *their* fear
that persists in this place, and will persist longer

than will the rusting metal
being taken by the miasma.

Our arms reach through the heart
of the thing. I perch every night

to watch the transformation of
the boy's gift, the car that was his

fleeting moment of control.
The smell of fear lingers

as branch after branch pierces through -
desperate, mindless, hungry.

I listen and I stare.
But I no longer hear the scream.

In Order Of Appearance:

Becca lives in Missoula, MT with her wife and kids. She teaches creative writing, but when she isn't doing that she is probably exploring or creating something. She is governed by insatiable curiosity.

Corie Rosen's work has appeared in Arts & Letters, Crab Creek Review, and Juked, among many other places. Corie's writing has also been anthologized, nominated for the Pushcart Prize, and featured on NPR. Corie's first book of poems, 'Words for Things Left Unsaid,' was published by Aldrich Press earlier this year and was nominated for the National Book Award.
You can find Corie on Instagram at @rosenbyanothername.

Quinton Jordebrek is an emerging transmasculine artist who currently resides in the Midwest. You can follow him on Instagrm @quinton_jordebrek

Alexx Mayes is a Los Angeles and Reno based photographer that specializes in the exploration of the human psyche, fusing the fundamentals of multiple disciplines within the field to create genre-defying art via multisensory mediums resulting in narrative-rich imagery. As a digital artist and videographer, she brings a layered approach to her work, capturing details with a myriad of perspectives.

Stella Robertson is a 19-year-old college student currently attending Portland Community College and working part-time at Village Merchants in Portland, Oregon. She has found her passion in creative writing and is excited to see where that passion will take her.

Laura Kenney (she/they) is a writer of poetry, nonfiction, and experimental texts; a film and digital photographer; and a conceptual artist. Her writing has been published in The Round, Ghost City Review, Clerestory Journal of the Arts, and elsewhere; and her lyric essay he/they/you/that/i: a testimony is the 2019 winner of the Frances Mason Harris '26 Prize. Laura can often be found sticking their nose into abandoned spaces, testing local library checkout limits, and writing about bifurcated tongues.

Grayson is a Black, queer transgender writer boi. He is a poet, moonlighting as a therapist. Grayson has been featured in Carnival Literary Magazine, Backbone Press and Belletrist Magazine. A Florida cowboy with a West Coast heart, he chooses madness: of the wild, of the truth, of love, and of dreaming. Choose madness. He hopes you can find some in his poems.
@_graysons_anatomy_

Gabriela De Paz is an artist from the San Francisco Bay Area. She works in a large variety of visual mediums including collage, painting, drawing, and photography. Her work is inspired by her emotions, particularly those she can't express in words. She currently resides in Valencia, Spain. You can find her on instagram @gabrieladepazart.

Shantha J. Bunyan, a Bi-POC, is a scuba dive master, currently land-locked in her native Colorado, USA. A former surgical technician, she holds a BA in Neuroscience from Colorado College. After giving in to her wanderlust in 2014, she lived abroad for nearly six years, traveling to over 35 countries, as she explored the world both above and below the surface. Sometimes she manages her chronic pain and invisible illnesses and sometimes they try to manage her; but while she's fighting, she writes. When she can't be in the ocean, she uses some of her rejected dive photos as backgrounds for found poetry she makes from various magazines and junk mailings. Her poetry appears in publications such as DoveTales, an International Journal of the Arts: Resistance, published by Writing for Peace; 140Max Magazine; What Rough Beast; Rigorous, The Silent World in Her Vase; Bluing the Blade by Tempered Runes Press; The Closed Eye Open; and From Whispers to Roars. Some of her travel adventures and links to her poetry can be found at RandomPiecesofPeace.com.

Trapper Markelz is a poet, musician, and cyclist, who writes from Boston, MA. His work has appeared or is forthcoming in the journals Baltimore Review and The Dillydoun Review. You can learn more at https://trappermarkelz.com.

Danny Rebb is a disabled self-taught photographer who first picked up a camera forty years ago and currently resides in Dearborn, Michigan. His work seeks to evoke emotion in the viewer by portraying unexpected beauty in overlooked places and circumstances as or to transform what at first glance seems to be grotesque into something beautiful.

Danny was previously published in Flora Fiction literary magazine. His work also appears on the cover of two poetry collections, All My People Are Elegies: Essays, Prose Poems, and Other Epistolary Oddities by Sean Thomas Dougherty, published by NYQ Books in 2019 as well as Portals: A Memoir in Verse by Nancy Owen Nelson, published by Kelsay Books in 2019.

Facebook: Danny Rebb Fine Art Photography
Instagram: @dannyrebbfineartphotography

Bingh studied literature and creative writing with Jim Crenner at Hobart College, where he founded and edited SCRY! A Nexus of Politics and the Arts (Anne Carson was among the contributors). From 2015-18, he wrote theater reviews for the San Diego Reader (under the name Binh H. Nguyen). Bingh holds an MFA degree in poetry from SDSU and is the founder, curator, and all-around impresario of Thru a Soft Tube, a monthly reading series in its fifth year in San Diego. His poems have recently received attention from The Common, Crab Orchard Review, HIV Here & Now, samfiftyfour_literary, Saving Daylight Zine, Poetry & Art at the San Diego Art Institute, the San Diego Poetry Annual 2020, and the San Diego Bards Against Hunger Anthology. You can find him at www.bingharoundthecity.com.

Christopher Ghattas is a biochemist with the CDC, though he also has a B.S. in English and enjoys writing whenever he has free time. His upbringing under an immigrant Greek father and large family afforded him with plenty of stories, from a childhood in South Carolina to France and back again. Travels and frequent moves inspired a love of visiting new places and photography.

Julia Gibson is a multidisciplinary thinker, creator, and problem solver aspiring to contribute to a more understanding and compassionate world. After studies in violin performance at Manhattan School of Music, she completed a BA in Cognitive Science at Brown University and an MSc in mathematics at McMaster University. She now works both as a poet and an aerospace engineer in Toronto. A supporter of pluralism and free speech, she is on the production team for Shab-e She'r, Toronto's bravest and most diverse poetry series. Her first full-length collection of poetry, Two Doors, was published in 2019 by Clare Songbirds Publishing House. Other of her poems have appeared or are forthcoming in Prairie Fire, Poetry Pause, Ink, Sweat and Tears, Vallum, and Wild Roof Journal.

Cheng Tim Tim is a poet and teacher from Hong Kong.

A native of Atlanta, Nichole Spates lived in New York City for eighteen years before moving to Orlando, Florida in 2019. Her photographic work, often shown or shared under the name LensMomentsNS, has increased in scope and volume over the last few years and reflects the incredible diversity of experiences that she encounters in her daily life. Her style is expressed through the lens of her personal interests which, beyond photography, include urban landscapes and parks, dance in nearly any form, nature- especially how it finds a way into even the most urban of environments, modern art and public art. Seeking out striking imagery through a lens has been a factor in her life since her teens. Her work has been shown in group exhibitions in New York City and Central Florida and featured in online group exhibitions and in print in a journal and an awards magazine.
IG: @nicholespates
Website: https://lensmoments643736928.wordpress.com

Andrew Tye is a full-time senior at Princeton University, currently in his hometown of Temple, Texas. His work has won the Morris W. Croll Prize and been published in The Nassau Literary Review. As an emerging writer, he is excited to share my passion for poetry. @andrewbltye

JoeAnn Hart is the author of Stamford '76: A True Story of Murder, Corruption, Race, and Feminism in the 1970s (University of Iowa Press, April, 2019), a true crime memoir. Her novels are Float (Ashland Creek Press, 2013) a dark comedy about plastics in the ocean, and Addled (Little, Brown, 2007) a social satire that intertwines animal rights with the politics of food. Her short fiction and essays have been published in a wide range of literary magazines and anthologies, including Prairie Schooner, The Sonora Review, The Hopper, The Woven Tale, Black Lives Have Always Mattered, and others. Her photography was exhibited in the Houston Center for Photography "Togethering" show, 2020. Her work, which also includes articles, essays, and drama, often explores the relationship between humans and their environments.
Instagram: @joeannhart76

Hannah Maureen Holden's short fiction has appeared in Cordella Magazine, Grody Mag, and The Ear. She is the founder of SLUG MAG, and serves on the fiction board of Columbia Journal. She lives and writes in New York.

Greg Turlock is a published poet, author and photographer. His credits include "Rivers of Life", award-winning poem from the 2019 Alberta Arts Awards, "Hightops in the Snow", his new young-adult novel, "Prairie Survivors" photo essay in High Shelf Press, cover photo for the Parkland Poets II Anthology and "Beauty from the Underworld" photo and poem in Tiny Seed Journal. Greg lives in Parkland County, Alberta CANADA www.gregturlockcreative.com

Josephine is a scientist by training, an educator by heart and a writer by nature. She lives in Oregon and frequently writes about invertebrates and trees. Her work has appeared in various journals including Fourth River, Raw Art Review, and High Shelf Press.

Highshelfpress.com